11/12

Anne Hathaway

BY DALE-MARIE BRYAN

The Child's World

Published by The Child's World®
1980 Lookout Drive • Mankato, MN 56003-1705
800-599-READ • www.childsworld.com

Acknowledgments
The Child's World®: Mary Berendes, Publishing Director
The Design Lab: Cover and interior design
Amnet: Cover and interior production
Red Line Editorial: Editorial direction

Photo credits
Featureflash/Shutterstock Images, cover, 1, 19; Walt
Disney/Everett Collection, 5; Seth Poppel/Yearbook
Library, 7, 9; PRNewsFoto/Walt Disney Pictures/AP
Images, 11; Adrian Wyle/AP Images, 12; Miramax/Everett
Collection, 15; Rex Features/AP Images, 17; Joe Seer/
Shutterstock Images, 21, 24; Mirek Towski/DMI via AP/
AP Images, 23; Music4mix/Shutterstock Images, 25; Jennifer
Graylock/AP Images, 27; Phil Stafford/Shutterstock Images, 29

Design elements
Sergey Shvedov/iStockphoto

ISBN 9781614732860
LCCN 2012933678

Printed in the United States of America
Mankato, MN
July 2012
PA02128

Table of Contents

CHAPTER 1

Klutzy Beginning

Being clumsy didn't stop Anne Hathaway from becoming a famous actress. In fact, Anne got her first big part because of it. Garry Marshall was the director for *The Princess Diaries*. He hired Anne when Anne fell out of her chair at the film's **audition**. Anne was hired for the part of the main character, Mia Thermopolis. The film was a big success.

Anne said a lot of the funny scenes of her character being clumsy were not in the script. The script is the written text for the film. "It was just me being a klutz," she said. A klutz is a person who is clumsy. Anne's first big role was playing a princess. Little did she know she would soon become a princess of Hollywood.

Anne Hathaway's first big movie role was in *The Princess Diaries.*

CHAPTER 2

Normal Childhood

Anne Jacqueline Hathaway was born in Brooklyn, New York, on November 12, 1982. Anne's mother, Kate McCauley, was an actress and singer. Anne's father, Gerald, was a lawyer. He once worked as a **stagehand**. Anne has an older brother named Michael and a younger brother named Tom.

Anne first went to Brooklyn Heights Montessori School. But she was raised in northern New Jersey. Her family moved to Millburn, New Jersey, when she was six. Anne went to Wyoming Elementary School there.

Anne's family and friends call her Annie.

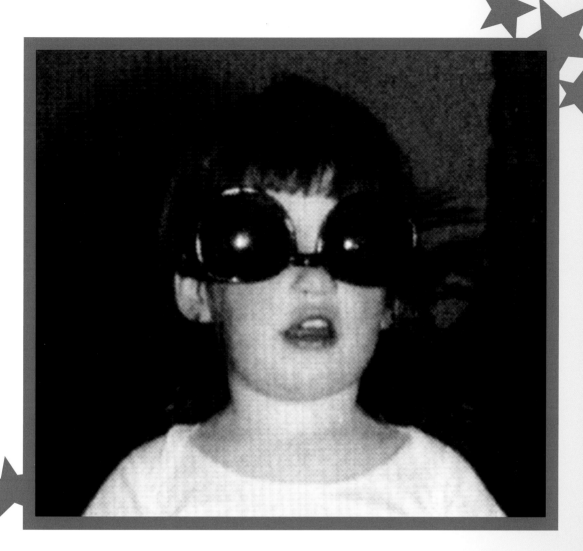

Anne as a young child

Anne liked to read growing up. She had a copy
of *Grimm's Fairy Tales* as a kid. She would stay up
late to read it. Some of the stories were violent. Anne
says she "used to love reading them with a flashlight

to freak myself out." One of her favorite stories was "The Fisherman and His Wife."

Anne became interested in acting at age three. She was traveling with her mother who was acting in a play. Anne's mother was touring nationally with the musical *Les Misérables*. Anne saw other young kids performing onstage. She wanted to be there, too. But Anne's parents didn't want her to start acting professionally yet. "They so wanted me to have a normal life as a kid," Anne said.

Anne in her first year of high school

CHAPTER 3

Playing a Princess

One of Anne's first times in front of a camera was in 1997. It was for a commercial for a real estate company. She had to cry in the commercial because her boyfriend was moving. At 16, Anne got a role on a television series. It was called *Get Real*. But it was canceled after one season.

Anne played a princess for the first time in a play in high school. She went to Millburn High School in New Jersey. She acted in a play called *Once Upon a Mattress*. Her famous role in *The Princess Diaries* led to even more princess roles. Anne went on to star in *The Princess Diaries 2: Royal Engagement* in 2004.

Anne with costar Julie Andrews at the opening of *The Princess Diaries 2*

Anne poses with her *Brokeback Mountain* costars.

She also played a princess in *Ella Enchanted*, which came out the same year.

Anne was afraid of being **typecast**. She was being asked to play the same kind of part over and over. Anne was growing up, too. She didn't want to only act in princess roles. So she decided it was time to take on more grown-up roles.

Anne also continued her schooling while she acted. After graduating from high school, she went to Vassar College in Poughkeepsie, New York. Anne studied English and Women's Studies. In 2005, she transferred to New York University in New York City.

In 2005, Anne was in the movie *Brokeback Mountain*. She played actor Jake Gyllenhaal's wife. The movie won many Academy Awards. In 2006, Anne acted with Meryl Streep. They were in the movie *The Devil Wears Prada* together.

Anne got the role of writer Jane Austen in *Becoming Jane* in 2007. In 2009, Anne was **nominated** for an Academy Award. The nomination was for her role in *Rachel Getting Married*. In the film she played a girl who is recovering from a drug addiction.

Anne also sings. She has performed at Carnegie Hall. Her singing training came in handy when she sang in *Ella Enchanted*. She has also sung at the Academy Awards. Once was in 2009. The other was in 2011, when she also cohosted.

CHAPTER 4

Hardworking Actor

Anne says keeping her energy level up is one of the hardest things about making a film. But she thinks her greatest quality as an actor is her belief in hard work. "I may not be the best in the world, but I love [performing] more than just about anything, and I will give everything I have to it," Anne said.

Anne has to prepare for her roles in many ways.

The only other job Anne ever had besides acting was babysitting. She didn't do very well. "I tried everything—singing songs, sprinkling fairy dust on her, everything—but this little girl did not like my bag of tricks!" Anne said.

Anne played writer Jane Austen in *Becoming Jane* in 2007.

Sometimes she has to read a lot. One example is when she was learning about writer Jane Austen. This was for her role in the movie *Becoming Jane*. Sometimes Anne has to learn to speak differently for a part. To play Jane Austen, she had to learn a British accent. Anne had to work with a language coach for six hours a day. For the same part, she also had to learn to play piano, dance, and write calligraphy. Calligraphy is a fancy and decorative way of writing.

For *Ella Enchanted*, Anne worked with a mime. Mimes act out characters or situations using only body movements. Anne had to learn how to make it look like someone else was controlling her body movements for that role.

Anne has also played Catwoman. That role was for the

Anne had a broken toe during the filming of *The Devil Wears Prada*. But she still had to wear very high heels.

Anne took stunt training for her role in
The Dark Knight Rises.

Batman movie *The Dark Knight Rises*. She had to be strong for that role. She had to work out five times a day. Anne also had to take **stunt** training and dance classes to prepare to play Catwoman.

Anne's work can be dangerous sometimes, too. One example is when she was filming the 2008 movie *Get Smart*. Anne was supposed to kick another actor for a scene. But she ended up kicking a metal bar. Anne had to have 15 stitches in her shin. She was also sick during the filming of that movie. There are many good things about being a famous actress. But Anne said one bad part is "you always have to work whenever you're sick."

Anne is a vegetarian. A vegetarian is a person who does not eat meat.

CHAPTER 5

Flair for Fashion

One thing Anne likes about show business is the fashion. She has been featured on the cover of famous fashion magazines. Two examples are *Harper's Bazaar*

Anne models a dress on the red carpet.

and *Vogue*. From 2006 to 2010 Anne was named one of *People* magazine's Most Beautiful People. But she doesn't take herself too seriously. When Anne made jokes during a *Vogue* photo shoot the photographer told her, "Anne—less talking, more beauty."

"I love [fashion] as an art form. I love it when people are able to [show] thoughts and feelings on fabric or some kind of material . . . I find fashion so fun," Anne said.

Even though she is part of the fashion world, Anne still enjoys being herself. Anne said she looks the best when people have worked on her hair and makeup. But she said she feels the best "when I haven't looked in a mirror for days, and I'm doing things that make me happy."

Anne has a chocolate Labrador named Esmeralda.

For Anne, fashion is a fun part of working in entertainment.

CHAPTER 6

Awards for Work

Anne has received many honors for her work. One was her Academy Award nomination in 2009. That was for her role in *Rachel Getting Married*. Anne was also nominated for a Golden Globe that year for the same film. In 2011, she was nominated for a Golden Globe again. That time was for her role in the film *Love & Other Drugs*.

Anne was also nominated for People's Choice Awards in 2009, 2011, and 2012.

In 2009, Anne was nominated for a Kids' Choice

Anne once said she wanted to work with director Tim Burton before she died. Anne got her wish. She was cast in the 2010 film *Alice in Wonderland*. Anne played the White Queen. Burton was the director of the film.

Anne has been nominated for many Teen
Choice Awards.

Anne poses on the red carpet at the 2011 Academy Awards.

Award. She was nominated for Teen Choice Awards in 2000, 2002, 2006, 2009, 2010, and 2011. She won a Teen Choice Award in 2009. The award was for the best movie actress in a comedy. It was for her role in *Bride Wars*.

CHAPTER 7

Giving Back

Anne believes in sharing her success with others. She gives her time and money to **charities**. One charity she gives to is St. Jude Children's Research

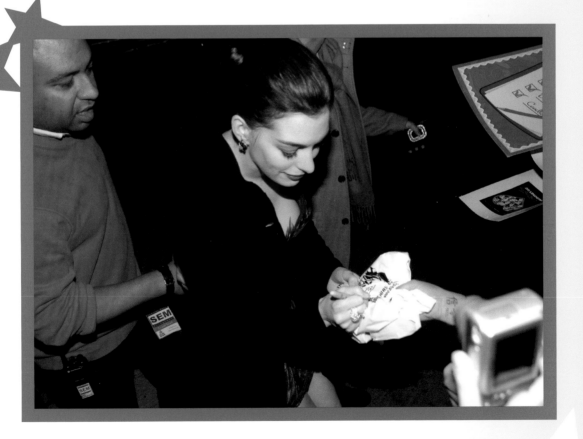

Anne signs autographs for her fans at a film showing.

Hospital. In 2006, Anne spent time helping kids in Nicaragua. Nicaragua is a country in Central America. While there, Anne helped give kids shots to prevent diseases.

Anne also works with the Lollipop Theater Network. This is a group that shows movies in hospitals for people who are very sick.

Another way Anne gives back is by setting a good example for her fans. "I really don't drink, I don't do drugs. I feel like . . . I've been given so many opportunities I don't want to mess it up," she said.

Anne wanted to keep her costume from *The Dark Knight Rises*. She wanted to visit sick children at the hospital dressed as Catwoman.

Anne supports several children's charities.

CHAPTER 8

The Future

In the future, Anne plans to keep acting. She would especially like to act in the musical *My Fair Lady*. "That's my dream role," she said. Anne also wants to work behind the scenes. She would like to work as a **producer** someday.

Anne has plans for her future personal life, too. She plans to marry and have a family. She also wants to try new things. Anne said she would like to try a little bit of writing, drawing, and shooting, which is photography or filming. She said, "I'd love to be an artist [with many talents]. At the moment, I am not . . . But I am a very hard worker and a very determined person, so who knows?"

Anne looks forward to a future of acting and trying new things.

GLOSSARY

audition (aw-DISH-uhn): An audition is when actors try out for a role in plays or films. Anne fell off a chair during her audition for *The Princess Diaries.*

charities (CHAR-i-tees): Charities are organizations that provide money or assistance to those in need. Anne likes to help children's charities.

nominated (NAH-muh-nate-id): To be named a finalist for an award is to be nominated. Anne was nominated for awards for her role in *Rachel Getting Married.*

producer (pruh-DOOS-ur): A producer finds the money to make a movie and supervises the making and distribution of the movie. One day, Anne may want to try work as a producer.

stagehand (STAYJ-hand): A stagehand works backstage to move scenery, handle lighting, and do other jobs during a production. Before he was a lawyer, Anne's father worked as a stagehand.

stunt (STUHNT): A stunt is an unusual or difficult physical trick that is done to entertain people. Anne had stunt training to play Catwoman.

typecast (TIPE-kast): To be typecast is to be given the same type of acting roles over and over. Anne was afraid of being typecast as a princess.

FURTHER INFORMATION

BOOKS

Cabot, Meg. *The Princess Diaries*. New York: HarperTeen, 2004.

Carroll, Lewis. *Alice's Adventures in Wonderland and Through the Looking-Glass*. London: Collector's Library, 2009.

Levine, Gail Carson. *Ella Enchanted*. New York: HarperTeen, 2004.

WEB SITES

Visit our Web site for links about Anne Hathaway: childsworld.com/links

Note to Parents, Teachers, and Librarians: We routinely verify our Web links to make sure they are safe and active sites. So encourage your readers to check them out!

INDEX

ABOUT THE AUTHOR

Dale-Marie Bryan is a former elementary teacher and the author of several books for children. She writes from the home she shares with her husband and many pets in southeast Kansas.